INVESTMENT IN IDOLATRY

poems by

Keith Moul

Finishing Line Press
Georgetown, Kentucky

INVESTMENT IN IDOLATRY

Copyright © 2017 by Keith Moul
ISBN 978-1-63534-100-3 First Edition
All rights reserved under International and Pan-American Copyright Conventions.
No part of this book may be reproduced in any manner whatsoever without written permission from the publisher, except in the case of brief quotations embodied in critical articles and reviews.

ACKNOWLEDGMENTS

Blazevox, "Talking Candy Bar Blues"
Burning Word, "Guilt by Implication," "Painted Face"
Calliope Magazine, "Collections"
Circleshow: Seven Circles Press, "Children at the Dreamscape"
Essence Poetry Magazine (Glasgow), "Political Float"
Eunoia Review, "Lesson: Confusion at the Root"
Poetic Reflections at the Creekside (Anthology), "A Distant Fire," "Speculations on Absences"
Straylight, "Moving On"
The Bitchin' Kitsch, "Mechanics Armed with Ancient Fire"
The Chiron Review, "The Hard Rain"
The Montucky Review, "Map of Scars"
The Write Room, "Spanish Cathedral"
Visions with Voices, "Collections"

Publisher: Leah Maines

Editor: Christen Kincaid

Cover Art: Keith Moul

Author Photo: Ianthe Moul

Cover Design: Elizabeth Maines

Printed in the USA on acid-free paper.
Order online: www.finishinglinepress.com
also available on amazon.com

Author inquiries and mail orders:
Finishing Line Press
P. O. Box 1626
Georgetown, Kentucky 40324
U. S. A.

Table of Contents

Moving On 1

"Talking Candy Bar Blues" 3

Children at the Dreamscape 4

Map of Scars 5

Images of Eight 7

A Distant Fire 9

Collections 11

One Day in Iceland, May 13

Spanish Cathedral 14

Painted Face 15

A New Intensity, Fire 16

Political Float 17

The Hard Rain 18

Leave It 20

Summertime in Great Falls 21

Government Man 22

Speculations on Absences 23

In a Hard Dream 24

Guilt by Implication 26

Dedicated to Sylvia, again and again

MOVING ON
> *I admit not knowing enough about my mother's life. Face to face,*
> *she not so subtly let me talk about myself. This is so easy for a son, to*
> *think that his success on the court is all that matters.*
> *(the funeral of Margaret Moul)*

You often said that you believed, that *your* mother's naked faith
pushed you into peopled conclaves such as bars and distant road houses,
an assortment of loud revelations. There you heard others shout out
their gaseous epics and the plausible deniability of immortality.

Today I talk over you, timidly, talk more about you than I ever did in life;
I share the bits that in my telling please me, mostly anecdotes about events
that seemed to animate your pleasures, your oddities and your kindnesses:

I am here as athlete to pay you homage, honorably falling short of oration.
But I may be right to infer, regardless of appearances, that faith was in you.
A few, probably the majority, would swear your faith heretical; would see
your face in smoky darkness, eyes cheered by bawdy sailors, tempers
 restrained
out of respect for your special loveliness; but would return with expectations
that Marge and Ralph may sometimes swirl, but to the very center of their
 fun.

Today we reach a compromise. Years notwithstanding, this thing must be
 justly done.
I follow in ceremonial procession, bearing my pall clumsily, but as best I
 can.

True, I invited expert witnesses to regale the mourners with your history,
 and desires.

Had such testament been forthcoming, this poem might have gone on for
 many pages.

And, what if all this fuss, the purple beads and pastel roses, the music from
 New Orleans,
the cool mother of pearl necklace, the stroll through the evergreens is
 unsuitable, all wrong?

You didn't leave instructions. You didn't seem to send your spirit on a *bon voyage!*

Long ago you didn't see me dunk a basketball. But you recognized my powerful spring.
I can't leap to greet you, I can't face your spirit, but my doubt may presage your immortality.

"TALKING CANDY BAR BLUES"
Noel Paul Stookey

In his deep, comedic voice, Paul Stookey sooloed with guitar a song about the evolution of innocence of boys and wickedness of adults, half a chocolate bar of unknown brand offered and neighbors near at hand policing street corners during public events. It escaped me but late news reported each detail in keeping with the fourth estate, without a hint of exaggeration, nor discernible whiff of fabrication.

Now I know the song by heart. The "angle" by the press is askew. Mr. Stookey was haplessly ensnared in a gangland conspiracy, set in motion by an innocent offer of "Candy, son," then shifting gear when the plainly scared boy returned with Mom and neighbors to say "Him!" Scared too, Mr. Stookey pretends to await the now late bus— "Anybody got a watch? You could see just how late it is. I got a better idea. Let's find somebody with a watch and stare at him."

Mr. Stookey must hear "Pervert, the kid's life is ruined," although he's now "IN THE MIDDLE OF A BUBBLEGU-U-M OR-R-GY!" (This capitalization and punctuation are mine for a "literary" effect.)

At top gear, racecar speed, Mr. Stookey has achieved enlightenment:

> Well, I've had some troubled times before
> but none like the trip from the candy store.
> Oh, I sympathize with the kid all right.
> Somebody's nice to you - probably ain't right.
> I'll grow up - I'll learn the way.
> I'll learn so that my later days will be pros-s-perous,
> chocolate covered - if I don't bite off more than I can hide.

You're right with me if you find the moral as well as the story immoral.

CHILDREN AT THE DREAMSCAPE
(coming to Christ)

What had the children heard?
Some heard snorting, maybe beasts,
maybe men, even crying as though cut
by sharp knives, but with many echoes.

What had the children seen?
Some recalled shattered images:
white lights; birds and angels shivering;
stubborn, frightful beasts with horns.

Children would not describe the smells.

No one could know for certain
as the telling of events differed,
as children feared even kindly listeners.

On feast days; lonely before icons;
while fighting with crude siblings;
hiding behind bushes from mean neighbors;
children quit their need for senses.

Often their parents reward them with halos.

MAP OF SCARS
    (thinking of DJ)

Here where trees blanch, boulders calve,
I feel the menace: branches spread
like steel spider webs wrapped in clouds.

You appear, sprung from close by, I think,
coiled, not buoyant
but strange to me.
                      Wind scours
this dying place where no stone,
no fallen leaf or gully rib
urges memory—
wind edges you toward me,
your hand reaches my hand:

murky, you can't be the man I knew.

Even this time is not my time;
your alien past intrudes.
How did you create this alien past,
your father's past, his history,
his violent facts,
his certain loss?

Dick, you ghost me to his trail;
your scars map his way to me.

You say his company stole his land,
this land, and chained the cabin door
that weathers white and grainy
like a bone, turns orange
with staining rust from links
and lock whose iron
would crumble now
if petted
by his living hand.

Materialize, Dick.
Vacate this brown, anonymous ditch
down which the summer rains,
given life, would plunge,
fit for drowning
or a final, frantic dance.

Live with me, Dick, both of us
treading history's hues and heft.

IMAGES OF EIGHT

Now nine, my daughter lives again
the images of eight at play,
seven at play, six, five, four…

her regression toward birth
of her life's brief dream,
her tri-color dinghy on the pond:
waking to it, another birthday makes her wise.

Or, so she says,
now grown up to talk with dad
of "interesting" things:
last night's sunset;
the world's best supermarket;
the ick of frogs;
or how effortlessly she steers
each shoal of passing childhood.

I follow her lead, tend her scrapes
(her scar migrates beneath her chin);
I dare her each adventure:
clearly, current arcs between her poles,
sparks light her way,
she grows within my sight
but outside my oft considered derangement.

I write the poem that limns her path,
posing *paterfamilias*, dreamer
of fitful dreams, tri-color of ignorance,
dire in confusion at the best of times:
my best poems
share this spirit.

Applaud it, and hers,
but forgive my daughter's innocence
of the poet's obscene will
that scares up bad poems
from mad corners of home.

A DISTANT FIRE

Not comfortable in society's give and take,
he had accepted as his first,
meaningful gift, death.

He felt uninvolved in the coming to,
as though life were a deceit,
a painful accident occurring to others
on the next street,
as though his children would be
equally distant from life's fire.

He was not young for death.
Certainly he had faced it
when young and escaped
perhaps buoyant in the Pacific.
But over time every door
and window opened onto death.
A screen of death surrounded
each relationship; tolls of death
were always being exacted;
rewards as accounts of others
not freighted by death were tallied.

At some point, lonely in life,
he craved society with death.

At the latest moment
he reacted to death,
assuming the fetal position,
refusing nourishment,
abandoning intellect and empathy.
He may have thought, if only
higher authority would intervene
with still another supernatural joke.

He had been up to death
for months. The bottom hours
toward his final cremation
quieted him.

COLLECTIONS

Unlike the Supreme Collector orchestrating His Genesis to scale,
I collected nicks and bits from mountains yielding to natural forces
without heaven at hand, nor a Master's plan (nor master race);
without ridicule by charmed fruit evoking a snake's evil will;
without two politicos in a room subverting freedom by spinning
seminal words assuming virtue; without capital more enormous,
always doubling, then always redoubling, double-dealing ad interim.

You've noticed that I began collecting as an innocent, looking down,
thinking small. Among knacks I found viper semblances needing venom;
fruit pits and seeds; leaf and branch symphonies in minor keys; vulgar
human tidbits spoiling in the common space; plastic jetsam tidal zones;
beastly boys and girls aping stupidly favored celebrities, but so unsavory.

I don't smoke, but I snatched a solitary matchbook from a hotel ashtray
in Bergen (when Ianthe convulsed while contracting *Salmonella*); I
snapped shots of middle Europe garden dirt, still aiming downward,
for Sylvia's scrapbook; I paid too much for the only baseball card
I had found for a ballplayer named Uhl, my mother's maiden name.

As a collector, I exult at lesser archives, never consulted or copied.

Others, sainted maybe, rush around greedily procuring bones
of near-saints from minor European cathedrals, long neglected;
some collectors worship whipped cream on chocolate, appeasing
mountain gods; some collectors lavish salt on their lips from mines
so deep, appeasing miners' gods, dangerously hostile to seasoning.

Some collectors partner in unseemly dance with demons of possessions,
that burrow through our reception antennae, darlings of hunger,
scavengers destructive of our sights, smells and sounds not bent on desire.

From the Grand Canal, for Venetian glass he'd sacrifice ever going home;
he'd scale Mt. Everest for a touch of glacier inching since the Pleistocene;
he'd purse his lips and bow to kiss the Devil's ass for *another* Mantle
   rookie card
with perfect corners, centered height and width graded "mint" by an
   honorable dealer.

See what a harmless hobby can become?

With my eyes straight forward, how could I expect to find *so* honorable a dealer?

ONE DAY IN ICELAND: MAY

Reykjavik shelters, but not coherently. People here fuse by nerve,
living leeward where trust becomes habitat. Arrivals and departures
hazard shearing wind at steep trajection to spite an indifferent ocean.

Beneath a rock bluff sits, freshly painted, a multi-colored house.
Supplies delivered recently included a new immigrant, the latest
excavators from Holland and a bountiful shipment of paints that
once in Reykjavik our man had to be content with three bent cans.

A circular highway and little side roads heading inland prescribe
a shackled to road surface route, "guiding" the adventurer in you.
I acceded to the obvious loop, always exploring from a roadside.

My travel fixes costs to new truths, such as this new landscape:
I am invested into terrain true only to the directions of the winds
that, as they shape hills and damn all scurrying life, ask fealty.
At light, alone on this landscape, unmarked in earth's rotation,
I consult map coordinates to fix a new scale for my anonymity.

Magnificence for my landscape; geothermal plume under my feet;
my voice confiscated as penalty by cursing winds come by again;
I navigate a moonscape early in its evolution, not yet engaging life.

SPANISH CATHEDRAL

No ceremony abets the spires;
they must stand on their own history.
A few minutes the bells are quiet;
their peal rumbles in the hills, however.
A wedding earlier has ended; white rose petals
trail on the breeze marking its dispersion.
No decorative crepe on the last tree
in the square; no crowds shuffle through the door
into the cool shade of the sanctuary.

For tourists like me, entry here is pedestrian only.
I consider the multiple meanings of the word:
depart on foot, observe this mundane life
circumscribed by eternal redundancy,
carry away with me buyer's Spanish, *amigo*.

Claim whatever beliefs you wish,
admire the Moorish arches, do not fear
an unforgotten burden of inquisition.

PAINTED FACE

Like a planet in a cold orbit, rarely
did he need the sun. *Stay on course,*
rotate at an awful pace, shed your ice

into the unlived silence of black space.
He fished catfish to see them dangle
helpless on a line. *Waste their fish souls,*

eat them panfried, wash them down with beer.
At private moments, with his lover in his arms,
he dreamed punishments for enemies.

Pile them on a heap, take your spoils,
mark your face with battle blood you won.
Passing within a whisper of home he did not hear.

Coming into old territory, he did not veer.
Leaving his mark on bushes, he felt gods in stars.
Take children in pairs, in ritual gag them, then watch.

A NEW INTENSITY, FIRE

> "I was glad the colonel had quit talking about fire. That had nothing to do with me."
> Sergeant Muldrow in To the White Sea by James Dickey

Beyond television spectacle, or
pyrotechnics in one action pic
after another, fire had consumed
only refuse at my mind's edge.

Anguish for the physics
of others' lives, often sparked
to private rage, was tabloid stuff.

Fire dynamic is clear:
oxygen, fuel, combustion source;
unerring predation of its object;
speedily forging furnace heat and,
if unconfined, chasing after holocaust.

For its light, alone first
in speed through the universe,
fire is now my certain element.

A new intensity assails my sinews,
new energy sparks the old synapses
adding danger in the mind
hurtling above fire-bombed Tokyo,
stealing my way toward magnetic north.

POLITICAL FLOAT

For a long time he worked at being just.
This was bad indeed for his digestion—
sour stomach amassed him no political capital.

He always aimed for truth: dead center demonstrably.
Too deep, he almost drowned in controversy.

He spoke too often of his hope in a little god
of charity; he cast his net in obscure seas;
he stumped so artfully to those bereft
that his opponent eschewed any coalition.

He came to regret freedom of speech as malicious
in the mouths of thugs and propagandists.

Before the election, he built a craft
uncomfortable for allies who read the winds
of a cold season, who knew clouds would rise
with a charge so electric it would part waves.

THE HARD RAIN

A bucket has completely filled
    with rain water.
Wind has driven the larger birds
    from local perches
    into hiding.
The purging dark of winter feeds
    onrushing apostasy
and there is no energy free for light.

For too many years I watched
    as a supplicant
    the natural night
alter into night imagined; I fought
    my unearthly bent;
I accepted a surreal parcel
    so often contested
in modern life, clogged by cholesterol.

But the *Concorde*, a supersonic
    mantis,
has done its time; cold to think
    of melting polar ice;
Coca-cola stands flat in a cup;
and pornography fills the internet,
    sans erotica.

More district attorneys take action
    against pedophiles
and domestic violence as more pedophiles
    and violent domestics enter our neighborhoods.

Rain thuds down like paratroopers
    to the eastern horizon
as morning returns to Americans
    their America,
faithful to investments in new ventures
    and idolatry.

LEAVE IT

Through years, each day like the mailman,
he lay wreathes at lovers' feet—
sentimental offerings to pink,
well-washed feet, not dancing.

For he did not dance, except
with common ideas of love,
not taking happiness by force: he
was clever, true, but largely unmoved.
He wasted early attempts at love.

Over and over he reached his conclusion,
the loneliness of inadequate effort,
the corruption of escaping gas;

not happy enough, clever but unmoved,
the kinds of objects that hide in corners
rather than be seen in unflattering poses,
all perfumed, stifling little sneezes;

>there are engines stinking of fumes too
>(pall overwhelms the entire track),
>the race is long, drivers rally and fall back
>as the winner glistens leading the pack.

SUMMERTIME IN GREAT FALLS

Mama fainthearted again stands by in a tremor, enduring
her pounding heart as mamas should; Sonny sits calmly
to observe the Missouri surging by with rising meanness,
brown whorls of silt, more eddies of lost fertility, more
eddies taken by eddies than there are forefathers' tears.

What have generations to do with learning? Do they pass
with current downstream? Do we learn from turbulence?

Flood warnings may be sounded and unheeded down stream
under the Plains' hot air, the sun blinding, progeny hot after it,
spending so little energy at the flood, design of the craft suffers.

Early sons left on important business. Later sons, inspired
by convenient technology, watched the falls' containment:
the flimsy craft could glide over smooth river surfaces all day.

Recent sons filled with manly ideas, unmoved by searing tantrums,
deny their mamas and rely absurdly on wayward boy's excuses,
after beckoning adventures: serious global wars, celebrations
of celebrity, crowning glories, anything to escape their loneliness,
the wages of sin if a position remains open: to avoid the flowing river.

GOVERNMENT MAN

The government man explains
to the press that sectarian hostilities
afflict that region of the world
and have for generations.
Killing there is second nature.

The government man explains
that Plan B will be applied
unless those in power bend
to the will of the powerless,
as represented by those even more
powerful. Meanwhile, killing continues.

The government man explains
that some minds are inscrutable,
that attitudes can be implacable,
so we too must be prepared
to kill if actual need arises.

Citizens of the world are encouraged
to send humanitarian aid promptly
as the dying continues out of all
proportion to self-interests
of concerned nations.

Tests are now being given
to fill a shortage of government men.

SPECULATIONS ON ABSENCES

I hadn't abandoned control.
As with an imperative tornado,
there is irksome damage
and pain of invasion.

Perhaps an uninvited but real guest,
arrived to share the moment,
including frustration with a bludgeon.

Glass shards gesture on the floor,
the smell of sweat—

there is a story to detect,
but apparently not of much good
as rarely good enters by force.

Perhaps an unknown intruder
has left me a crude version of reality.

My windows have been covered
and no additional complaint has been made.

IN A HARD DREAM

Waking, I hear rushing away an almost known voice.
I hear my father, Ralph, who could bark, but rarely,
start his loud diesel truck, scatter gravel and leave
for Memphis on his regular run, but he is dead now
twenty-five years (perverse silence): his is not the voice.

Often in dreams I am visited by his father, Grandpa Jim,
deft with chisel and Wisconsin stone for monuments when
builders featured cut stone to embellish more than real need.

Although Grandpa Jim could rant at the "ornery" ways of men,
he rarely spoke above a raspy whisper. Jim is dead fifty years,
that I would not vouch for his voice: his is not the voice I hear.

I conjure these men's last days to find a likely source of counsel:

one day in St. Louis, without attendance, dad died disinterested,
fatally ill, but mostly overwhelmed by angst and failed marriage.
He maneuvered his truck over scripted terrain, in command, but
without a subordinate, perhaps singing falsetto, but I doubt it.
He fought a Pacific war, starting on top, but often swept below
huge swells, dogpaddling after life and certain entitlements, but
not to salvation beneath the public address, nor otherwise significant.
His doctors, his nurses, monitored his going among hospital gong.

Grandpa Jim had sharpened his tools and hung them neatly oiled
on his cool basement wall, carved and fitted stone quarried near Lodi.
Stones in or out of a quarry may chorus together, but do not speak.
Jim later sat in a second story hallway outside an apartment, with door
and windows open for cross-ventilation; he too not otherwise significant.

Dad wrote a war journal to his wife, who found him otherwise insignificant.

Perhaps in his final delirium, dad called upon his father Jim for help
and the voice I hear are confused, receding words of my own delirium
as fine, even as true as can be expected late in life in a hard dream.

GUILT BY IMPLICATION

A man came to my door
claiming witness to atrocities
committed on my behalf, but
in places I had never been.

He said I was duty bound
as a citizen beneficiary—
whether on hillsides of poppies
bodies explode, or not—
to stand behind our rightful leaders.

He offered digital images for sale,
un-enhanced, if I preferred.
If I preferred, guilty charges
made first in ancient texts
illustrated by monks, could be had—
actually his biggest seller—all certified.

I sent him away.
   I alerted friends to his scam.
     But, I checked local news in case;
published articles did appear,
but made no local accusations.
In fact I inferred implicit guilt.

Amazed,
   I could not disprove any atrocities
     on any dates cited
        by any surrogates
           killing thousands in my name.

Confused, I went to the mountains.
Heavy snow fell, drew me in,
quietly deep. I shook, although relieved.
The National Geographic
reports deprivations in deep
snow abet atrocities.

Keith Moul was born 3 months after VJ Day. His father, Ralph, served on aircraft carriers in the Pacific in World War II, and Keith developed a strong interest in U.S. history growing up at that particular time. He's always writing his poems, taking his pictures and studying reliable historians to understand his times.

Keith was born in St. Louis and is a life-long Cardinal fan. Baseball fills capably the long, hot, humid evenings in St. Louis. Not fast enough for baseball, he turned to schooling in literature: the U. of Missouri, AB '67; Western Washington State U., MA '71; 1972 at the U. of Iowa where he studied Old English; and U. of South Carolina, PhD '74.

He married Sylvia in 1967 and they remain very happily together. His daughter, Ianthe, was born in 1969 and has blossomed into a compelling artist in paints.

But most of Keith's time since leaving school has been spent in the commercial insurance world, employed by various companies in underwriting, marketing and underwriting management. He was retired in 2001 due to company mergers, a destructive practice among financial businesses.

But the administrative part of poetry has become significantly more possible with the advent of computers and the internet. This book was submitted, reviewed and accepted by Finishing Line Press as an electronic transaction; so was *The Future as a Picnic Lunch*, which FLP published in 2015.

All this amounts to an interesting life of pleasant retirement.

www.ingramcontent.com/pod-product-compliance
Lightning Source LLC
LaVergne TN
LVHW051613080426
835510LV00020B/3280